Flowers
for
Forrest

by

Jonathan S Baker

Salish Sea, International Waters

Copyright © 2023 Jonathna S Baker

Pretty please, don't steal our words, or we will shimmy up your toilet, wiggle into your stink-hole, and use you as a vertebrate puppet. You will do our bidding and catch us very many tasty shellfish. Also, if you like copying other people's writing so much, you should have no problem copying illuminated medieval manuscripts in Latin by hand with a quill. Doesn't seem so glamorous, now does it? Please enjoy this book as you will, quote it as often as you wish, and lend it out at your leisure, but DO NOT claim it as your own or produce unauthorized editions, or so help us Neptune, we are going to crack you open like a clam.

First Edition: 1 3 5 7 6 4 2 8 8 8 8 8 8 8

ISBN:979-8-88596-441-8

Design, Layout, and Edits: Paul "The Psychic Octopus" Schreiber
Interior Photos: Antoine Vladimir Ball
Cover: Antoine Vladimir Ball

"Parody is Satire gone sour."
-Brenden Gill, American Journalist

    The following is printed as parody please take it as seriously as you may. All images have been pilfered from the public domain.

Foreword

I'm Forrest, Forrest Gump

Forrest Gump Looks Back on How He Got into School.

Magic Shoes for My Mind.

I Got to Meet the President, Again.

She taught me

Brood Parasite

I Gotta Find Bubba

I Was Running

She Ran, Too

No Warnings

Foreword

On *Flowers For Forrest*, I had little idea what to expect from this book of poetry that explores a popular movie character's inner dialog, but I assure you, no way did I expect such totally absorbing brilliance.

Jonathan S Baker takes a fascinating excursion through the consciousness of Forerst, Forrest Gump. This slim volume is absolutely a must-read. And that is all I have to say about that!

> Dean McClain author of *Spiltsville* and *Exit, Netherville*. He is a woodcarving artisan specializing in fishing lures used by a wide variety of anglers from weekend casters to pros on the BASS tournament circuit. He is also a friend.

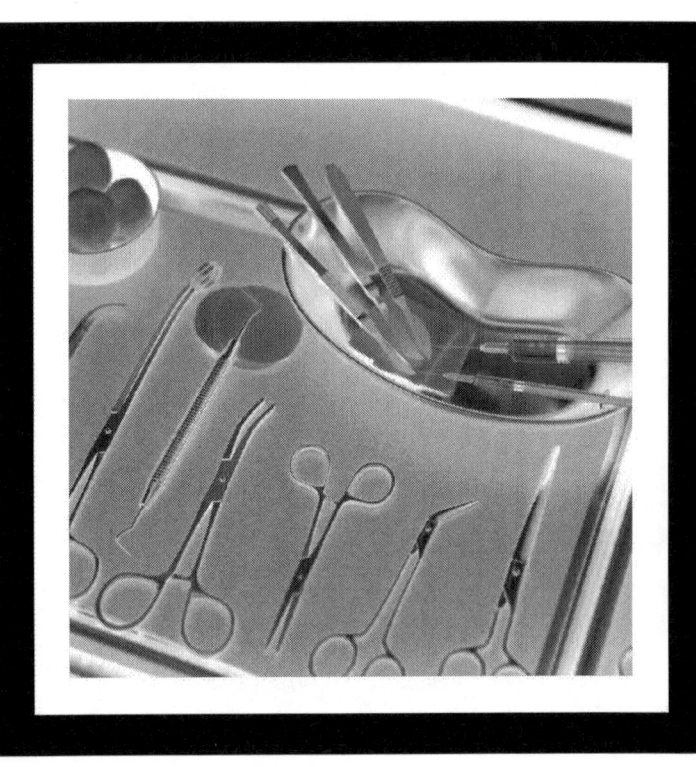

I'm Forrest, Forrest Gump

Something bit me
right there by that river in Vietnam.
Bubba died, I got to go home.
I fell asleep.
Alice wakes me.
She tells me she is a teacher
for special people like me.
She must mean soldiers,
because I'm in an army hospital.
I got shot in the buttock
but Professor Nemur
wants to operate on my brain.
Stupid is as Stupid does.
Who is Charlie Gordon?
Alice says he is gone.
Mama what's "vacation" mean?
My head hurts.
I'm scared too, Bubba.
I want to go home.
Who is Algernon?
Alice says he is gone.

Forrest Gump Looks Back on How He Got into School.

I knew what they were doing in there.
I know what a man and a woman do
when they go in the bedroom.

Forever after that he would watch me in the halls of the
school and I knew.
I knew he was thinking of Mama.

Some of the big boys in school talked
about what Mama done with the principal.
They said she would do it for a nickel.

I thought about Mama and the principal.
It made me feel dirty and tight.
I wish I could undo that night.

Magic Shoes for My Mind.

Lieutenant Dan! Ice cream! Lieutenant Dan! Ice cream!

They twisted off the top of my skull like a soda pop.
POP!

They poked around in there to see what I would do.
They showed me pictures and had me say the words.
There was a picture of a woman, and I said "Mama."
There was a picture of a coffin, and I said, "Bubba."
Pictures of men, boats, mountains, cars, tits, soldiers,
burnt bodies, and the like and it just went
on and on nearly forever.

They took a big old scoop to make some room and put in
some wires and tubes just like in the television set in
mama's front parlor room.

The lights went flashing.
I gotta pee.
Lieutenant Dan! Ice cream! Lieutenant Dan! Ice cream!

Please put the top of my head back on. I'm getting cold.
They said it was a billion dollar operation.
I don't know nothing about that.
The government must keep that money
because I ain't seen a penny.

I wanted to tell Lieutenant Dan
all about the surgery,
but when I came back to my bed
they told me he had gone.

I Got to Meet the President, Again.

When I met President Kennedy,
I wasn't smart enough
to consider doing
what that man in Dallas would do.
I was just excited to be on the TV
and drink all them Dr. Peppers.
By the time I met President Johnson,
I was smart enough
and close enough
and trained in what to do
but deep down I knew
it wouldn't change
the state of things.
I take a bit of solace
in having showed him
my ass.
Just a side note,
when I heard about Chapman
I had to choke down a laugh.
Imagine that you arrogant prick.
Nixon wasn't all that bad
at least he didn't get Bubba killed
or laugh at me.

She taught me

That night in her room
when I ruined her
roommate's robe
she taught me
a lesson I studied
again and again
at a massage parlor
called the Viking in Vietnam,
a lesson I returned to
with a thousand women
at truck stops and motels
along the roads.
She taught me
what I wanted,
what I needed,
to give myself over
complete and total
to release myself.

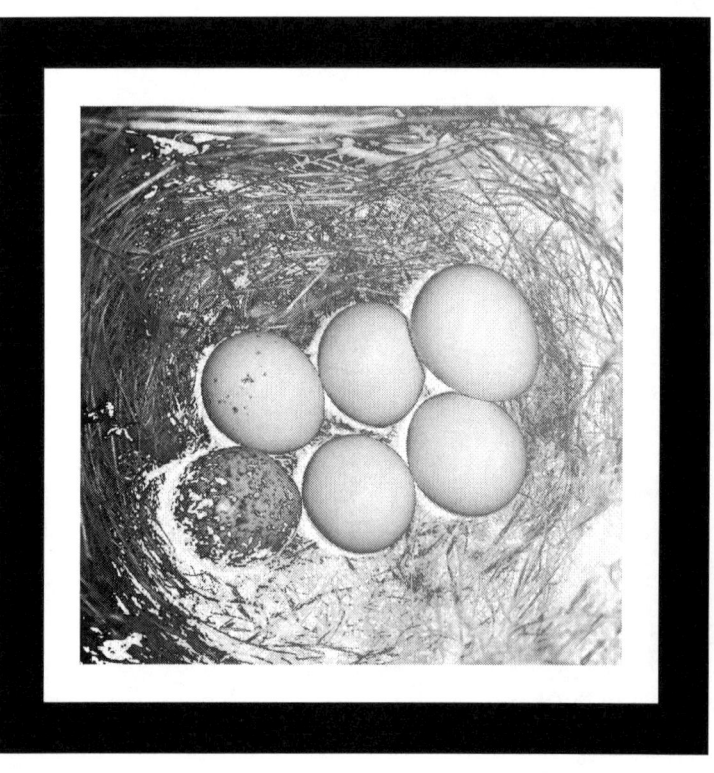

Brood Parasite

Back when Jenny and me prayed
for god to turn her to a bird
so she could fly far far away.

He did.

She wasn't no dove or chickadee.
She was a cuckoo
dropping her egg in my nest
for me to raise.

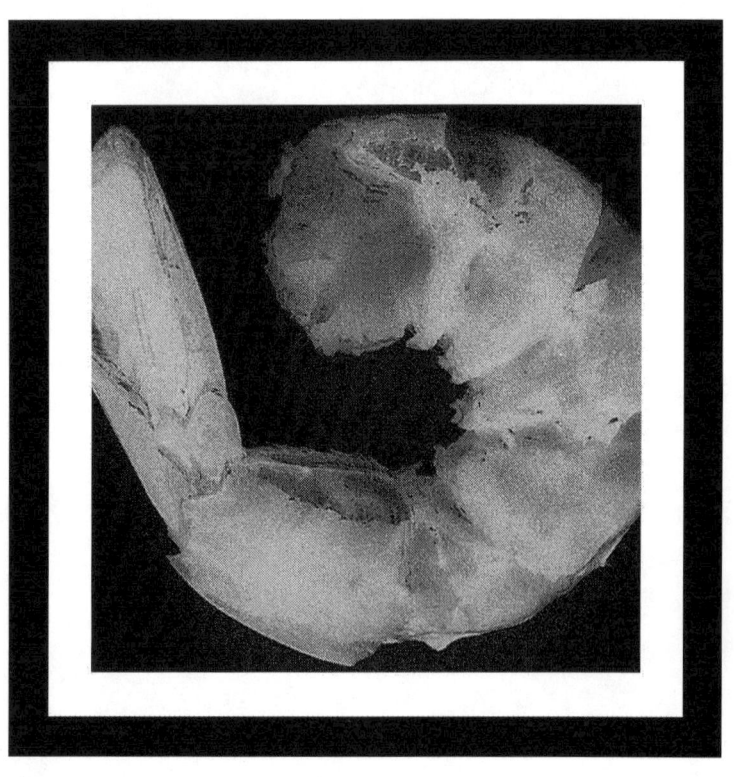

I Gotta Find Bubba

When I got back
after the war
I looked for you in Alabama
I looked at your Mama's
and at the church.
I think I saw you once
during a storm
while Lt. Dan was screaming
like a mad man
up on the mast
cursing God.
I saw you out in the storm
on the water
with your lower lip hanging.
I missed you brother.

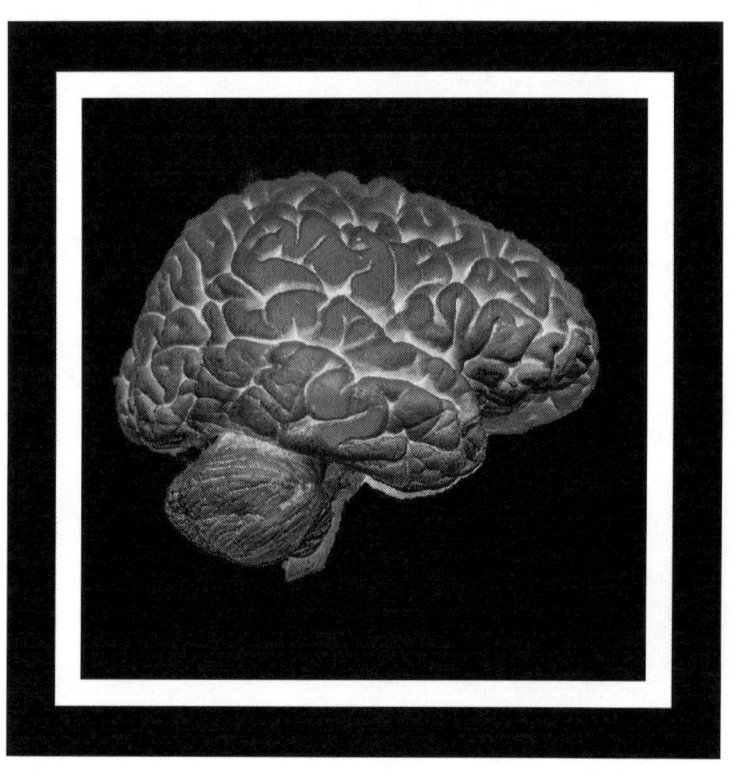

I Was Running

Before I started running,
I could feel it slipping away.
I was trying to figure out
why Jenny left
and it felt like I had
a cage clamping down
on my mind
just like those damned shoes.
Mama called them my magic shoes.
Back when I ran
from them boys
throwing them rocks
I unlocked my legs.
I could run and I was fast.
I was a runnin' fool.
So when she left
I was running to save my mind
to shatter the cage
before it returned.
I just felt like running.

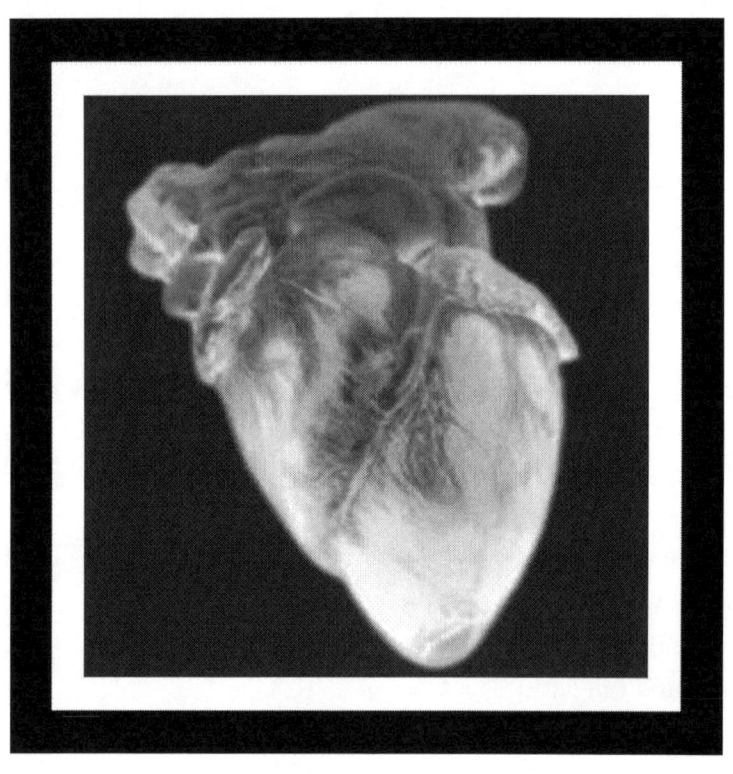

She Ran, Too

When we were kids
and the boys threw rocks at me,
she told me to run.
So, I ran.
I would do whatever she asked.
Again, when I ran from
those boys almost men
in their truck,
it was for her.
If i did it my way
I would have climbed in that truck
and beat those boys almost men
like I did that night I went
to see her.
I ran in the jungle
to save Bubba but
it was for her.
Everytime she could have loved me
she ran, too.
We never got to run together.

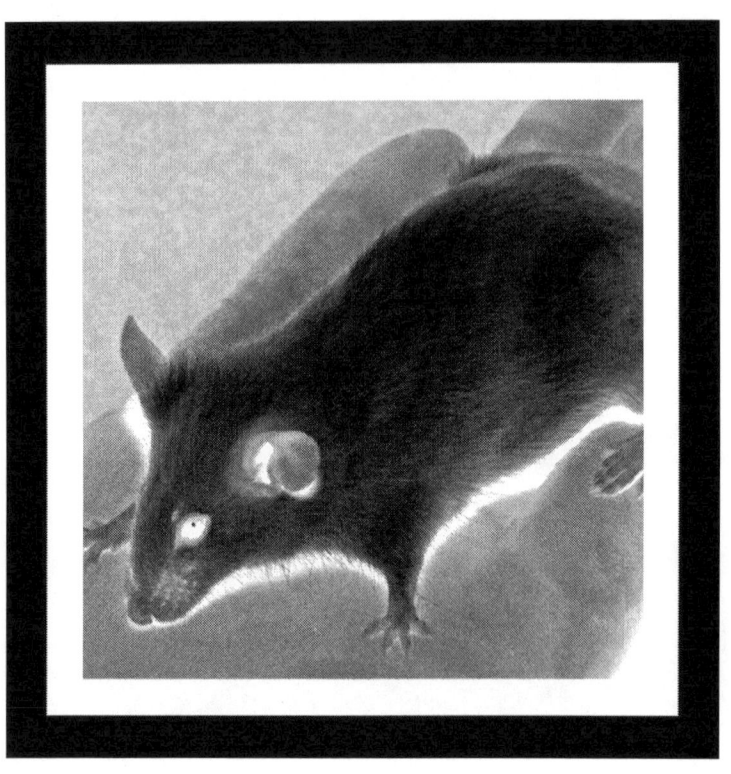

No Warnings

Charlie Gordon disappeared.
Algernon stumbled in the maze
and died spitting and angry.
He saw the darkness coming.
I have no such alarms to warn
of my decline.
There was no mouse this time.
So I just keep running
through my days
worrying that I might stumble
and harm the boy.

Jonathan S Baker lives in Evansville, Indiana where people are very particular about their Christmas Trees and is the author of several collections of poetry including *Cock of the Walk* (Laughing Ronin Press), *Long Nights in Stoplight City* (Between Shadows Press), and *Preassure* (Two Key Customs). They are also the host of Poetry Speaks, Indiana's longest running and most prestigious poetry reading.

jonathan.s.baker@gmail.com

Made in the USA
Columbia, SC
28 November 2023